Avenues
Program Guide and Assessment Handbook

LEVEL A

Acknowledgments
Hampton-Brown extends special thanks to the following individuals and companies that contributed to the creation of this component.

Development Team
Illustrators: Nan Brooks, Ginna Magee, Corasue Nicholas, Russell Nemec, Marian O'Neal.

Editorial: Renee Biermann, Janine Boylan, Susan Buntrock, Julie Cason, Esther Kim Choi, Lisa Cittadino, Honor Cline, Phyllis Edwards, Roseann Erwin, Kristin FitzPatrick, Nadine Guarrera, Margot Hanis, Fredrick Ignacio, Cynthia Keith, Phillip Kennedy, Tiina Kurvi, Dawn Liseth, Daphne Liu, Sheron Long, Guadalupe Lopez, Jackie Mahler, Michele McFadden, Steven Newitt, Amy Ostenso, Heather Peacock, Michael Priestley, Ann Seivert, Elizabeth Sengel, Jessica Sevey, Juan Quintana, Sharon Ursino, Andrea Weiss, Barbara Wood, Cullen Wojcik, Virginia Yeater.

Design and Production: Laurie Albrecht, Mary Ann Andrews, Renae Arcinas, Christy Caldwell, Sherry Corley, Wendy Crockett, Darius Detwiler, Jeri Gibson, Terry Harmon, Davis I. Hernandez, Rick Holcomb, Martina Hopkins, Ernie Lee, Connie McPhedran, Russell Nemec, Marian O'Neal, Anthony Paular, Deborah Reed, Cathy Revers, Debbie Saxton, Curtis Spitler, Jonni Stains, Kim Svetich-Will, Debbie Wright Swisher, Andrea Erin Thompson, Donna L. Turner, Vicki Vandeventer, Alex von Dallwitz, JR Walker, Marcia B. Walker.

Cover Design: Pronk&Associates.

Copyright © 2004 Hampton-Brown

All rights reserved.

Teachers are authorized to reproduce the assessment materials contained in this Handbook in limited quantities and solely for use in their own classrooms.

Other than as authorized above, no part of this book may be reproduced or transmitted in any form or by any means, electronic or mechanical, including photocopying, recording, or by an information storage and retrieval system, without permission in writing from the publisher.

Hampton-Brown
P.O. Box 223220
Carmel, California 93922
1–800–333–3510
www.hampton-brown.com

Printed in the United States of America

ISBN 0-7362-1819-X

07 08 09 10 11 12 9 8 7 6 5 4

Contents

▶ **Effective Education for English Learners** by Dr. Eugene García T4
▶ **Assessment Overview** T10

Progress Tests

Mid-Year Progress Test
  Directions 2
  Student Profile 5
  Test 6
  Answer Key 16

End-of-Year Progress Test
  Directions 19
  Student Profile 22
  Test 23
  Answer Key 33

Performance Assessments

Vocabulary Assessments 38
Language Assessments 48
Concepts of Print Assessment 52

Student Profile: Year-End Summary . . . . inside back cover

Avenues to Success

Effective Education for English Language Learners
by Eugene E. García, Ph.D.

English Language Learners Today

As we look at the students in our classrooms, we see a picture much different from the classrooms of our childhoods. According to the 2000 U.S. census, approximately one in three schoolchildren is from an ethnic or racial minority group, one in six speaks a language other than English at home, and one in ten is born outside the U.S. The linguistic and cultural diversity of the U.S. school population has increased dramatically during the past decade and will continue to increase. The concept of "minority group" will soon become obsolete, with no one group being a majority.

Educating children from immigrant and ethnic-minority families is a major concern in school systems across the country. Administrators, teachers, parents, and policymakers urge each other to do something different—change teaching methods, adopt new curricula, allocate more funding. Such actions might be needed, but they will not be meaningful until we think differently about English language learners.

A New View of English Language Learners

We are acutely aware that many English language learners come from families that are poor and non-English speaking. Too often, we have viewed these students only from the perspective of what they need to learn and from what they don't have. We need to move from this needs, or deficit, approach to an asset-inventory approach. That is, we need to perceive students' native language and culture as resources, or assets, instead of as problems. Students acquire language, culture, and accompanying values in the home and community environment and bring these assets with them to school.

In the past, when we have focused solely on the teaching of the English language, students received instruction to improve their English with the false understanding that learning English was all they needed. English language learners are capable and deserve the same access to the content standards as mainstream students.

These students do, however, need specialized instructional strategies that will ensure both their access to the standards and their success in achieving those standards. Specialized strategies for English language learners include:

- an interactive environment in which students constantly communicate for authentic purposes

- frequent opportunities to share and connect their prior knowledge and experiences to their peers' knowledge and to the academic content being studied

- multi-level activities and sheltering techniques to allow students at every level of English proficiency access to grade-level concepts and vocabulary

- assessment that tests students in the way they have been taught. That is, teachers assess student progress at benchmark proficiency levels—Beginning, Intermediate, and Advanced—in order to see progress on academic standards even as students move through the stages of language acquisition.

This new view has profound implications for the education of linguistically diverse students. It argues for the respect and integration of students' languages, values, beliefs, histories, and experiences. It argues for increased rigor and higher expectations—all supported by specialized instructional strategies. And it recognizes the active role that students must play in their own learning process.

Effective Education, continued

The New View in Practice

My wife, Erminda García, put this new view into practice in her third-grade classroom at Alianza Elementary School in Watsonville, California. At the beginning of the year, she asked students to consider this thematic study: "Three R's: Resourcefulness, Responsibility, and Respect." Students considered how they could become resourceful, responsible, and respectful in relationship to each other and to what they had to accomplish in the classroom.

Students' languages were immediately identified as resources. Students then articulated the ways in which other resources (parents, family, books, computers, etc.) could be used to enhance their academic pursuits.

For example, Rigoberto came to Erminda's classroom in September, after having arrived from Mexico in the last two months of the preceding academic year. A note in his file indicated a set of academic weaknesses. Erminda's first set of inquiries addressed what Rigoberto brought as resources. She asked him to talk about himself, his family, his community, and his educational experiences orally with her and in an interactive journal using his languages.

This asset inventory allowed her to place Rigoberto in the best academic circumstances, so that he could serve as a resource to others, and to maximize the classroom resources that could be made available to him. That made him an immediate participant in his own and his peers' education.

Knowing Rigoberto's resource portfolio allowed Erminda to modify instruction in ways that would support his learning. She began moving him from his native language in his journal into comfortable and skilled writing in English. Knowing what he could do in one language gave her a set of possible instructional "avenues" that she could use to develop English expertise.

Erminda also structures her classroom for interactive learning. She organizes desks in ways that promote the sharing of students' language resources: children sit in groups of four, with desks facing each other. Even in whole-group instruction, children are paired for interactive response. During instruction, students select from resource materials in English and native languages, often using each other for assistance in selecting those materials. Examples of learning are always put on display in whatever language the learning was accomplished, whether those resources are published works, brainstorm charts, or actual student products.

Finally, Erminda and all of her school colleagues established content benchmarks for each grade level and then assessed student work on a regular basis. The teachers used these ongoing assessments to identify both strengths and weaknesses; then, they could use specific instructional links to increase student learning. In this classroom, like other effective classrooms we have studied, there is always a concern for instruction focused on the articulated standards and ongoing assessments of student learning.

Guiding Principles for Curriculum, Assessment, and Instruction

The theory, research, and practices described above can be summarized in a set of North Star principles that can guide the work of educators serving English language learners. The North Star does not tell a traveler the precise way to travel. It does, however, provide an unwavering and ever-present indicator of the traveler's location in relation to the journey. The following guidelines are meant to inform your classroom journey toward academic success for your English language learners.

The languages and experiences of the student and her or his family and community are recognized and respected.

Curriculum and assessment sometimes ignore students' primary languages, even when primary language instruction is a major aspect of the program. And too often instruction based on a mainstream curriculum suffers from a mainstream approach. For example, English language learners are sometimes asked to write about vacations or travel; many students—especially those in urban or poor schools—cannot meaningfully participate in such an activity. Teachers need to choose reading material and instructional activities that are more intrinsically interesting, relevant, and motivating for English language learners.

High standards are the basis for curriculum, instruction, and assessment.

Most school districts and states have articulated English language arts standards. Standards make clear the expectations for students' skill level at each grade. Therefore, curriculum, assessment, and instruction for English language learners must reflect and be aligned with the standards; specialized instructional strategies, delivered by quality materials with built-in supports, must provide these students access to those high standards.

Effective Education, continued

⭐ *Assessment is on-going and makes progress visible even as students move through the stages of language acquisition.*

Standardized tests given to students in the spring are not intended to inform instruction, since results of such tests are not distributed or discussed until the fall. Standardized tests have their place in an accountability system, but they are not and should never be understood as the best way to assess specific student needs or to indicate instructional changes required to address the needs.

Instruction needs to provide feedback that informs instruction; therefore, it is imperative that such assessments occur at regular and strategic times during the year and that teachers test what they are teaching and in ways that reflect that teaching. Since most classrooms have students at varying levels of language proficiency and since teachers must use specialized strategies to teach those students, it follows that assessing student learning must be a multi-level activity. Teachers then have access to rich information regarding students' learning on a continuous basis.

Moreover, instruction can be modified to target specific student needs, which have been made visible by the multi-level assessment. Of significance, too, is the development and growth information that becomes available. Theoretically and empirically, we have come to understand that language and literacy development is not linear, that it can be unique to each student. Regular assessment allows us to maximize instructional opportunities.

⭐ *Teachers are able to use assessment results to inform, adapt, and maximize language and literacy instruction.*

Assessment that is "usable" provides information about performance on specific standards in language and literacy. It provides multiple products—authentic products as well as numerical scores—that allow teachers to verify students' language and literacy engagement. Usable assessment also makes progress visible and lets the teacher see and explore trends for an individual student, as well as for groups of students. And finally, usable assessment identifies specific instructional strategies for reteaching, which helps individual students develop in specific areas.

⭐ *Students are actively involved in the development and implementation of the instructional process.*

The older and more mature the student gets, the more that student is able to be a partner in the teaching and learning process. Students can meaningfully participate in their own education by:

- contributing their prior knowledge to the study of new topics
- examining their own work and sharing their reflections
- reviewing and even expanding on their mastery of the local and state standards. Teachers should always consider it important to let students know the expectations and to provide them with numerous models of student work.

In this manner, students become part of the process and assume a role in assessing their own learning.

Conclusion

These guiding principles, much like the North Star directs a night traveler, can give important insights into curriculum design, instruction, and assessment. Following these principles is beneficial to all learners, but imperative in the delivery of high-quality, standards-based instruction to our linguistically and culturally diverse students.

You will find that the curriculum design and instruction in *Avenues* reflects these North Star principles, and the *Avenues* **Assessment Handbook** provides assessment tools that yield usable results, across the many domains of literacy. Use these tools to monitor student progress across the year and use the results to inform your teaching.

ABOUT THE AUTHOR OF THIS ARTICLE

Dr. Eugene García is Vice President for University-School Partnerships and Dean of the College of Education at Arizona State University. He has received numerous academic and public honors and has published extensively in the area of language teaching and bilingual development. He holds leadership positions in numerous professional organizations and regularly serves as a panel reviewer for federal and state agencies. He served as a Senior Officer and Director of the Office of Bilingual Education from 1993–1995 and continues to conduct research in the areas of effective schooling for linguistically and culturally diverse student populations.

Assessment Overview

Program Goals

The goal of *Avenues* is to move English learners through the stages of language acquisition, while providing comprehensive, standards-based instruction at each child's level of language proficiency. The chart below summarizes the skills in *Avenues*.

Avenues Scope and Sequence Strands

Program Level	A	B	C	D	E	F
Language Development and Communication	•	•	•	•	•	•
Language Functions	•	•	•	•	•	•
Language Patterns and Structures	•	•	•	•	•	•
Concepts and Vocabulary	•	•	•	•	•	•
Reading	•	•	•	•	•	•
Learning to Read: concepts of print, phonemic awareness, phonics, decoding, and word recognition	•	•	•	•	•	•
Reading Strategies	•	•	•	•	•	•
Comprehension	•	•	•	•	•	•
Fluency		•	•	•	•	•
Literary Analysis and Appreciation	•	•	•	•	•	•
Listening, Speaking, Viewing, and Representing	•	•	•	•	•	•
Cognitive Academic Skills	•	•	•	•	•	•
Learning Strategies	•	•	•	•	•	•
Critical Thinking	•	•	•	•	•	•
Research Skills	•	•	•	•	•	•
Strategies for Taking Tests		•	•	•	•	•
Writing	•	•	•	•	•	•
Handwriting	•	•	•	•	•	•
Writing Purposes, Modes, and Forms	•	•	•	•	•	•
Writing Process		•	•	•	•	•
Writer's Craft		•	•	•	•	•
Grammar, Usage, Mechanics, Spelling	•	•	•	•	•	•
Technology and Media	•	•	•	•	•	•
Cultural Perspectives	•	•	•	•	•	•

Assessment Tools to Inform Instruction

Avenues provides an array of assessment tools that allow you to diagnose, monitor progress in language and literacy, and sum up yearly progress for each child.

Assessment Tool	Description	Diagnosis	Progress Monitoring	Summative
Progress Tests	Use these tests to assess children's mastery of standards in vocabulary and comprehension / critical thinking.		✓	✓
Vocabulary Assessments	These performance assessments measure children's progress in acquiring unit vocabulary.		✓	
Language Assessments	These performance assessments measure children's facility with the functions of language.		✓	
Concepts of Print Test	This performance assessment lets you see children's progress in reading readiness.		✓	

Avenues offers lessons in *Alphachants*™ for a complete scope and sequence of beginning phonics skills. Assessment tools in the *Alphachants* **Teacher's Guide** allow you to evaluate mastery of phonics and decoding skills.

Assessment Tool	Description	Diagnosis	Progress Monitoring	Summative
Phonological and Phonemic Awareness Assessment	This test measures a child's ability to identify rhyme, isolate sounds, blend sounds and segment words, and manipulate sounds.	✓	✓	✓
Letter-Sound Assessment	This test measures the accuracy and fluency with which the child gives the sound for each letter. It also evaluates knowledge of letter names and key words for each sound.	✓	✓	
Progress Tests	Five tests measure the child's phonological and phonemic awareness and knowledge of letter-sound correspondences to determine readiness for decoding lessons.		✓	
Posttests	This multiple-choice, group-administered test assesses the phonics skills and decoding skills taught in this program.			✓

Progress Tests

Purpose and Description

The **Progress Tests** are multiple-choice measures of children's performance in these primary domains:

- **Vocabulary** Measures children's understanding of the content vocabulary taught in the preceding five units.

- **Comprehension / Critical Thinking** Evaluates children's use of comprehension and critical thinking skills taught in preceding units.

- **High Frequency Words** This optional subtest can be administered to Advanced learners as a way to assess their mastery of each unit's high frequency words.

Administering the Tests

Administer the **Mid-Year Progress Test** after you have completed Units 1–5; administer the **End-of-Year Progress Test** after you have completed Units 6–10. Make a copy of the test for each child, or use the consumable test booklets available separately from Hampton-Brown. Use the directions for each test that appear before the test pages in this Assessment Handbook. The directions include complete scripting for working through sample items. Give children as much time as they need to complete the items in a subtest.

Scoring the Tests and Reporting Results

Tests can be scored by hand or machine. For hand-scoring and reporting, follow these steps:

1. Record results on the **Student Profile**. Write the child's name and test date at the top.

2. Use the **Answer Key** to score the test. Circle the item number of each correct answer. Compare the number of correct answers to the number given for Mastery. If the number correct matches or exceeds the Mastery number, circle the plus sign (+). If not, circle the minus sign (–).

3. Then multiply the number correct by the points per item to calculate the score for each subtest. Finally, add together the scores to find the total test score.

For machine-scoring and reporting:

1. Have children mark their answers on the test pages. Transfer their answers onto the *Avenues* machine-scorable answer sheets, which are compatible with Scantron™ and other standard scanning technologies.

2. After you scan the completed answer sheets, use *Avenues* e-Assessment to score the tests and generate reports.

Student Profile, Level A Mid-Year Progress Test

Student Profile • Mid-Year Progress Test

DIRECTIONS Record the child's name and test date. Use the **Answer Key** on pages 16–18 to score the child's test. Then, in the Student Profile, circle the item number of each correct answer and circle the plus or minus sign to indicate mastery. Calculate the subtest scores and then the total test score.

Student Name: Kim-Ahn N.   Date: 12/10

Subtest	Tested Skills	Item Analysis — Item Numbers	Mastery	Test Scores — No. Correct × Points = Score
VOCABULARY	Vocabulary from Units 1–5	①②③④⑤ ⑥⑦⑧⑨⑩ 11 ⑫	10 out of 12 ⊕ −	11 × 5 = 55/60
COMPREHENSION	Comprehension and Critical Thinking	13 14 ⑮ ⑯	3 out of 4 + ⊖	2 × 10 = 20/40
			TOTAL MID-YEAR PROGRESS TEST	75/100

FOR ADVANCED STUDENTS:

LEARNING TO READ	High Frequency Words	17 ⑱ ⑲ ⑳ ㉑	4 out of 5 ⊕ −	

MASTERY

Kim-Ahn met the Mastery criterion for Vocabulary. She answered 11 out of 12 questions correctly.

She did not meet the criterion for Comprehension, so the minus sign is circled.

SUBTEST SCORES

The subtest score equals the number of items correct multiplied by the number of points per item. Kim-Ahn's score for the Vocabulary subtest is 55/60.

Vocabulary Assessments

Purpose and Description

Level A of *Avenues* is designed to build children's vocabulary in 40 common kindergarten topics. To assess how children are doing in acquiring each unit's vocabulary, use the Vocabulary Assessments at the end of each unit. There is one performance assessment activity per vocabulary topic; each activity utilizes an *Avenues* program component with which children are familiar.

Conducting the Performance Assessment

Form groups of four children, while the other children are working independently or with peers at centers. After the suggested warm-up, carry out the activity, listening for each child's use of the unit vocabulary. Circle each word the child can point to or say in response to your prompts. Record additional unit vocabulary words used or other observations as you listen. For example, you might note when a child is mostly responding to Beginning-level prompts or when a child starts responding with single words or phrases (an Intermediate level) or when she or he produces a fluent sentence in response to your prompts (an Advanced level).

Assessment Overview

Vocabulary Assessment Form, Level A Unit 4

Circle each word the child points to or says in response to your prompts.

Unit 4 • Vocabulary Assessment

DIRECTIONS Set up the activities described on Teacher's Edition page T176, at the end of Unit 4. Then form small groups. After you record each child's name, carry out the activity. Listen for children's use of the unit vocabulary and circle each word a child can point to or say in response to your prompts. Record additional comments.

Places		Date 11/10	Workers		Date
Name	Vocabulary	Comments	Name	Vocabulary	Comments
Kim-Ahn	(post office) (restaurant) (fire station) (bakery) (grocery)	Kim-Ahn said each word.		doctor nurse letter carrier firefighter baker	
Julia	(post office) (restaurant) fire station (bakery) grocery	Julia pointed and didn't know all the words.		doctor nurse letter carrier firefighter baker	
Ben	(post office) (restaurant) (fire station) bakery (grocery)	Ben used each word in a sentence.		doctor nurse letter carrier firefighter baker	
Juan	(post office) (restaurant) (fire station) (bakery) (grocery)	Juan gave details about each word.		doctor nurse letter carrier firefighter baker	

Opposites		Date	Safety Words		Date
Name	Vocabulary	Comments	Name	Vocabulary	Comments
	back/front full/empty open/closed over/under up/down			stop look listen crosswalk green light	
	back/front full/empty open/closed over/under up/down			stop look listen crosswalk green light	
	back/front full/empty open/closed over/under up/down			stop look listen crosswalk green light	
	back/front full/empty open/closed over/under up/down			stop look listen crosswalk green light	

Make notes about how the child is responding.

Language Assessments

Purpose and Description

Level A of *Avenues* is also designed to help children become familiar with and start producing developmentally appropriate functions of language. One or more language functions are taught in each unit and are then recycled throughout the program. Language Assessments may be administered in an on-going fashion, after the unit in which the function is introduced, or as part of a grading period. Be sure, however, to take regular assessments so that you can monitor progress effectively and collect at least 5 or 6 assessments across the year for each child.

Conducting the Performance Assessment

Work with pairs of children. Model the function and conduct the activity. Check the box in the Language Proficiency Rubric that most closely matches your observation of the child's performance.

Interpreting Results

As you accumulate several Language Assessments for each child, you should begin to see a pattern emerge. For example, for children who are clearly at the beginning stage of English language development, you will find that the Beginning box is usually checked. This will enable you to tailor instruction to children's individual levels of language proficiency using the Multi-Level Strategies in the Teacher's Edition.

As a child makes progress in language development, you will begin to note that you are checking off the Intermediate or Advanced boxes more frequently. Once the assessments begin to indicate increased proficiency, begin using teaching ideas from the Multi-Level Strategies that reflect the child's higher proficiency.

Assessment Overview

Conduct the Language Assessment any time after the unit in which the language function was introduced.

Language Assessment Form, Level A

Name Kim-Ahn N.

Language Assessments

LOOK AT THE CAR GO!
USE AFTER UNIT 3

Date 10/30

- **Language Function:**
  Give and Follow Directions
- **ACTIVITY:** Display a toy car and truck or the **Vehicle Manipulatives** from Unit 3 on a table or desk. Say: *Hold up the car. Put the car on the desk. Push the car across the desk.* Then have each child give you directions. Check the box in the Rubric that most closely matches your observation.

Rubric
- ☒ **BEGINNING** Moves the car appropriately to show understanding of the directions. Uses gestures or pantomimes to give directions.
- ☐ **INTERMEDIATE** Successfully follows the directions and uses simple sentences with a few errors to give directions *(Hold up car. Put on desk. Push.)*.
- ☐ **ADVANCED** Accurately follows the directions and repeats them or gives new directions with few or no errors.

ARE THEY ALIKE OR DIFFERENT?
USE AFTER UNIT 4 OR 5

Date 11/30

- **Language Function:**
  Make Comparisons
- **ACTIVITY:** Display two red crayons, one shorter than the other. Ask children: *How are these the same?* (Both are red. Both are crayons.) *How are the crayons different?* (This/That one is shorter/longer.) Check the box in the Rubric that most closely matches your observation.

Rubric
- ☐ **BEGINNING** Uses gestures or single words to identify points of comparison *(red, crayons; short, long)*.
- ☒ **INTERMEDIATE** Uses simple phrases with comparative words and few errors *(Both red; red crayons; is shorter)*.
- ☐ **ADVANCED** Uses complete sentences and comparative words *(Both crayons are red. This crayon is shorter than that crayon.)*.

TELL ABOUT THE ANIMALS
USE AFTER UNIT 6

Date _____

- **Language Function:**
  Give Information
- **ACTIVITY:** Display the animal manipulatives from Unit 6. Have each child choose an animal. Then say: *Tell me the name of your animal.* (Pause.) *Tell me one thing it has. Tell me what it is like.* Check the box in the Rubric that most closely matches your observation.

Rubric
- ☐ **BEGINNING** Points to and names the animal. Points to one feature (ears, tail, etc.) and acts out what the animal is like.
- ☐ **INTERMEDIATE** Uses short phrases and simple sentences with a few errors to name the animal and give information about it *(Fish. Has fins. Little.)*.
- ☐ **ADVANCED** Uses complete sentences with details to give information about the animal *(This is a giraffe. It has a long neck. It is tall.)*.

USING THE RUBRICS

On October 30, the Beginning box is checked off because Kim-Ahn answered with gestures. A few weeks later, she was able to respond with short phrases that showed comparisons. That is why the Intermediate box is checked.

Student Profile: Year-End Summary

Purpose and Description

The **Student Profile: Year-End Summary** is where all of the assessment in *Avenues* comes together. The form provides you with a snapshot of each child's cumulative performance in Vocabulary, Comprehension and Critical Thinking, and Language.

To fill out the form, review the collection of test results and performance assessments from the year.

❶ Progress Tests Student Profiles
For each test, transfer the scores.

❷ Language Assessments
Review results on the Language Assessments (see pages T16–T17) and summarize the child's language growth. Comment on progress through the levels of English proficiency and command of an increasing number of more complex language patterns and structures.

❸ Vocabulary Assessments
Review the completed Vocabulary Assessments (see pages T14–T15) for how many words the child has acquired and for your observations about how the child was able to demonstrate vocabulary acquired across the year.

Determining Adequate Yearly Progress

As a final step, complete the **Yearly Progress** box to indicate growth in proficiency level across the year.

- Record the starting date and the initial proficiency level based on the results of your state- or district-approved proficiency instrument.

- Then consider growth in proficiency level indicated by performance on the **Language Assessments**.

- Consider all the information you have to determine the ending proficiency. Then circle the appropriate level and date the form.

Student Profile: Year-End Summary, Level A

Teacher **Mrs. García**   Student Name **Kim-Ahn Nguyen**   Date **May 15, 2004**

Student Profile: Year-End Summary

PROGRESS TESTS

DIRECTIONS Refer to each **Progress Test Student Profile** to record children's scores.

	MID-YEAR PROGRESS TEST SCORE	END-OF-YEAR PROGRESS TEST SCORE
VOCABULARY	55	60
COMPREHENSION / CRITICAL THINKING	20	35
STUDENT TOTAL	75 /100	95 /100
HIGH FREQUENCY WORDS	4 /5	5 /5

PERFORMANCE ASSESSMENTS

Language Assessments

DIRECTIONS Review the completed assessments and look for:
- progress through the levels of language proficiency
- command of an increasing number of more complex language patterns and structures.

Your observations:
Kim-Ahn is still shy about talking, but when she does, she often speaks in complete sentences.

Vocabulary Assessments

DIRECTIONS Review the completed assessments and make notes about the child's progress.

Your observations:
Kim-Ahn loves to learn new words!

Concepts of Print Assessment

Final Test Score: 12 /15; 75 %

Your observations:

YEARLY PROGRESS

DIRECTIONS Review state- or district-approved standardized test results and circle the child's initial proficiency level. Then review the **Language Assessments** and circle the child's current level.

Started **Aug. 15** as Ⓑ Ⓘ Ⓐ
          (date)

Ended **May 15** as Ⓑ Ⓘ Ⓐ
          (date)

CONTINUING SUPPORT

The Year-End Summary can travel in the child's cumulative folder. These observations will give Kim-Ahn's next teacher a fuller picture than test scores alone can.

ADEQUATE YEARLY PROGRESS

One form sums up yearly progress at a glance.

Progress Tests

▶ **Directions**

▶ **Student Profiles**

▶ **Progress Tests**

▶ **Answer Keys**

Units 1–5 • Directions for Mid-Year Progress Test

Administer this Progress Test in 2 or 3 sessions, based on the attention span and level of your students—**Session 1:** Vocabulary; **Session 2:** Comprehension; **Session 3:** High Frequency Words. Administer the test on High Frequency Words only to advanced students who are learning to read in English.

Distribute pencils or crayons for circling answers. Draw a star on the board to help children locate the place to begin.

VOCABULARY

Distribute pages 6–10. Say:

Sample
Put your finger on the star. Look at the pictures in the box. Find the crayon…crayon. (Pause.) The first picture is the crayon. That's why there is a circle around the crayon.

Items 1–12
Use the locator art to direct children from item to item. Repeat the directions using these prompts. Allow time for children to circle their answers.

1. *Find the table…table.*

Have children go to the next page.

2. *Find the crossing guard…crossing guard.*
3. *Find the mother and the baby…mother and the baby.*
4. *Find the sandwich…sandwich.*

Have children go to the next page.

VOCABULARY continued

5. *Find the spoon…spoon.*
6. *Find the bus…bus.*
7. *Find the triangle…triangle.*

Have children go to the next page.

8. *Find the supermarket…supermarket.*
9. *Find the doctor…doctor.*
10. *Find the girl who is raking…raking.*

Have children go to the next page.

11. *Find the rainy day…rainy day.*
12. *Find the tree in the fall…fall.*

Units 1–5 • Directions for Mid-Year Progress Test

COMPREHENSION

Selection 1 and Items 13–14

Distribute page 11. Have children look at the page and follow along as you read the story. Direct children from picture to picture. Say: *Now listen to the story. The title is:*

What Can I Wear?

Look at Picture 1.   I can wear a jacket and pants in the fall.

Look at Picture 2.   I can wear mittens, boots, and a sweater in the winter.

Look at Picture 3.   I can wear a raincoat and rain boots in the spring.

Look at Picture 4.   I can wear sandals and a sundress in the summer.

Distribute page 12. Say:

13. *Put your finger on the book. Now look at the sandals. The girl can wear sandals in the summer. What else can she wear in the summer? Can she wear a sundress or boots? Find what she can wear in the summer. Circle your answer.*

14. *Put your finger on the chair. Now look at the mittens. The girl can wear mittens in the winter. What else can she wear in the winter? Can she wear a raincoat or a sweater? Find what she can wear in the winter. Circle your answer.*

COMPREHENSION continued

Selection 2 and Items 15–16

Distribute page 13. Have children look at the page and follow along as you read the story. Direct children from picture to picture. Say: *Now listen to the story. The title is:*

Stop, Look, and Listen

Look at Picture 1.   See the children.

Look at Picture 2.   See the crossing guard. See the crosswalk. See the children stop, look, and listen.

Look at Picture 3.   See the children walk. See the car go!

Distribute page 14. Say:

15. *Put your finger on the pencil. Listen to the question:* What happens first in the story? *Look at the pictures. Circle the picture that shows what happens first.*

16. *Put your finger on the ball. Listen to the question:* What happens last in the story? *Look at the pictures. Circle the picture that shows what happens last.*

Units 1–5 • Directions for Mid-Year Progress Test

HIGH FREQUENCY WORDS

Distribute page 15. Say:

Sample
Put your finger on the star. Read the words. Find the word it. *Listen: I like* it. (Pause.) *The last word is* it. *That's why there is a circle around the word* it.

Items 17–21
Use the locator art to direct children from item to item. Repeat the directions using these words and context sentences. Allow time for children to circle their answers.

17. I...*I am happy.*
18. and...*We run and jump.*
19. the...*Look at the dog.*
20. you...*You can read.*
21. see...*I see a cat.*

Units 1–5 | Directions

Student Profile • Mid-Year Progress Test

DIRECTIONS Record the child's name and test date. Use the **Answer Key** on pages 16–18 to score the child's test. Then, in the Student Profile, circle the item number of each correct answer and circle the plus or minus sign to indicate mastery. Calculate the subtest scores and then the total test score.

Student Name _____ Date _____

Subtest	Tested Skills	ITEM ANALYSIS		TEST SCORES
		Item Numbers	Mastery	No. Correct × Points = Score
VOCABULARY	Vocabulary from Units 1–5	1 2 3 4 5 6 7 8 9 10 11 12	10 out of 12 + −	_____ × 5 = ⬚/60
COMPREHENSION	Comprehension and Critical Thinking	13 14 15 16	3 out of 4 + −	_____ × 10 = ⬚/40

TOTAL MID-YEAR PROGRESS TEST ⬚/100

FOR ADVANCED STUDENTS:

Subtest	Tested Skills	Item Numbers	Mastery
LEARNING TO READ	High Frequency Words	17 18 19 20 21	4 out of 5 + −

Units 1–5 | Student Profile

Name _____

LEVEL A

Mid-Year Progress Test

VOCABULARY

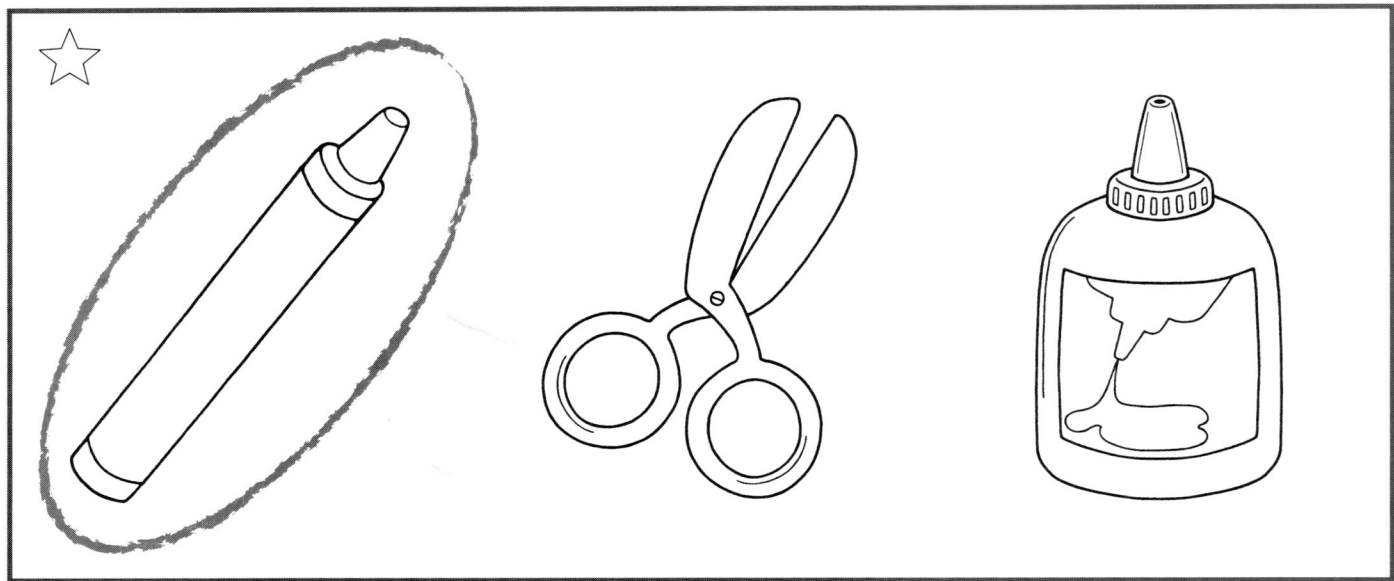

1 📕

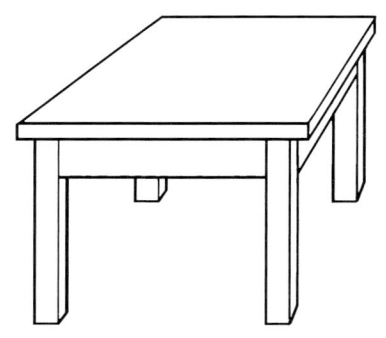  

Units 1–5 | Mid-Year Progress Test

6

Name _____   LEVEL A

VOCABULARY

2

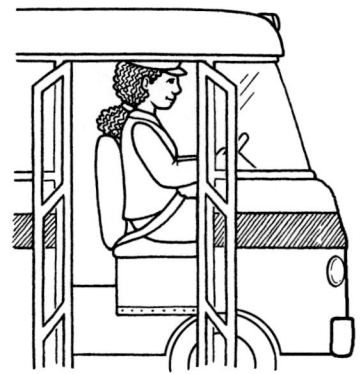  

3

4

 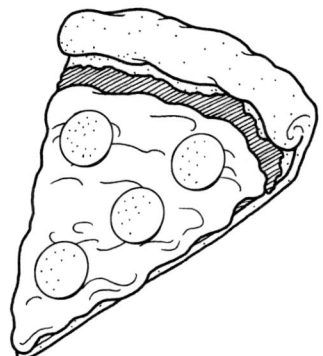 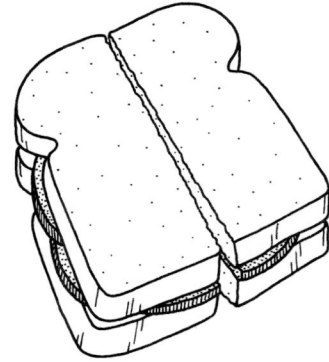

Units 1–5 | Mid-Year Progress Test   7

Name _____

LEVEL A

VOCABULARY

5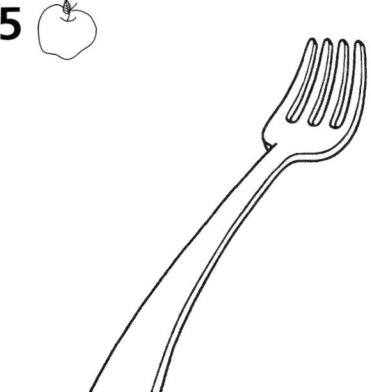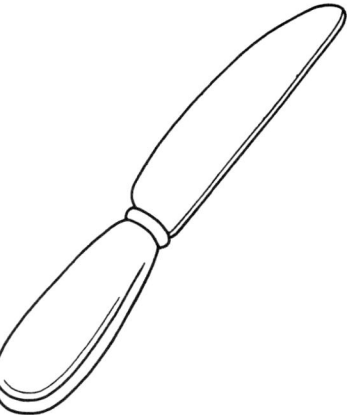

6

7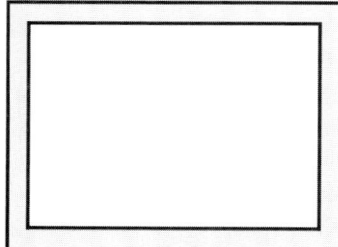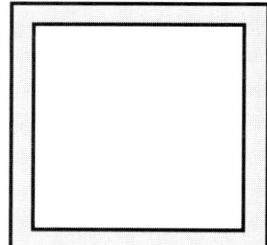

Units 1–5 | Mid-Year Progress Test

Name _____   LEVEL A

VOCABULARY

8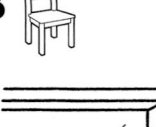

9 ✏️

10 🏐

Units 1–5 | Mid-Year Progress Test   9

Name

LEVEL A

VOCABULARY

11

12

Units 1–5 | Mid-Year Progress Test

What Can I Wear?

Name

LEVEL A

COMPREHENSION

13 📖

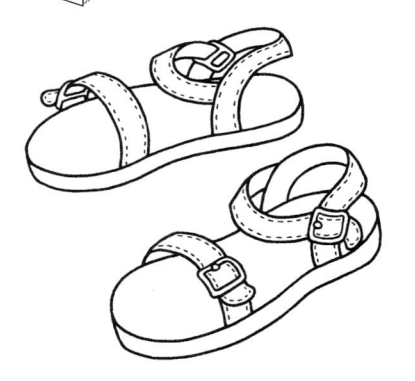  

14 🪑

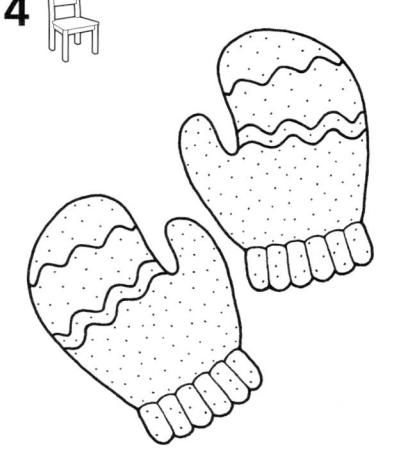  

Units 1–5 | Mid-Year Progress Test

Name _____   LEVEL A

COMPREHENSION

Stop, Look, and Listen

1

2

3

Units 1–5 | Mid-Year Progress Test

Name

LEVEL A

COMPREHENSION

15 ✏️

16 🏐

Units 1–5 | Mid-Year Progress Test

STOP

Name _____ LEVEL A

HIGH FREQUENCY WORDS

☆	the	a	(it)

17

in	I	at

18

and	can	see

19

this	to	the

20

you	and	we

21

to	see	is

STOP

Units 1–5 | Mid-Year Progress Test

Answer Key • Mid-Year Progress Test

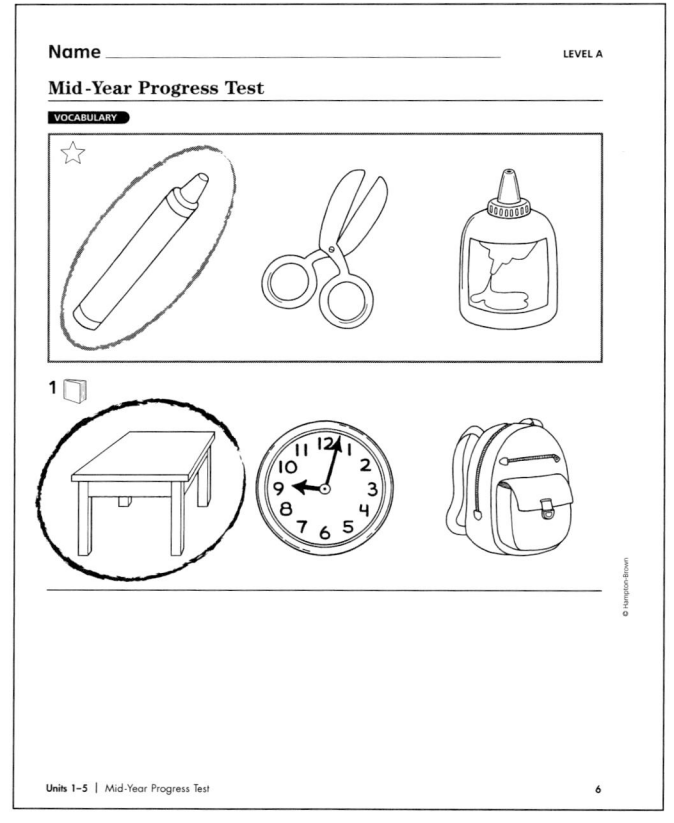
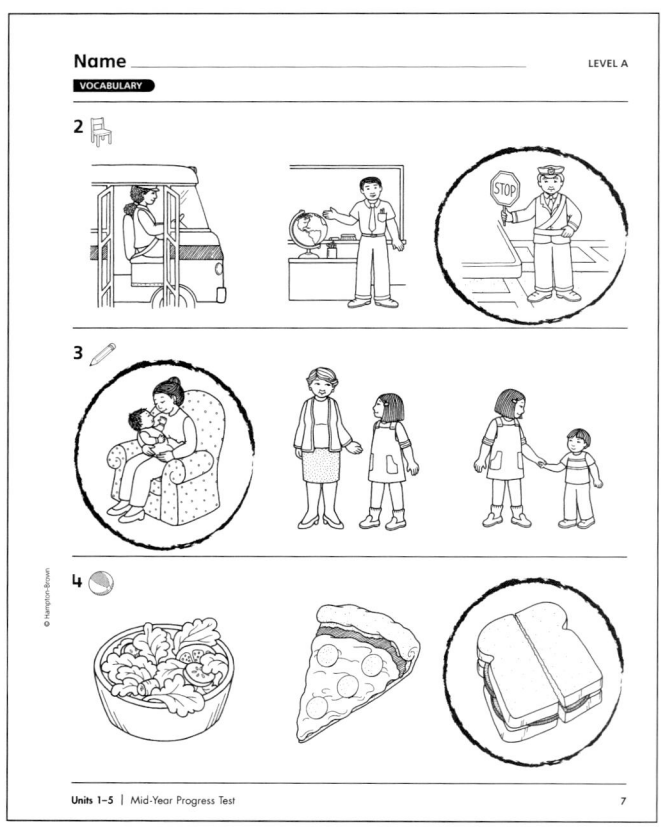
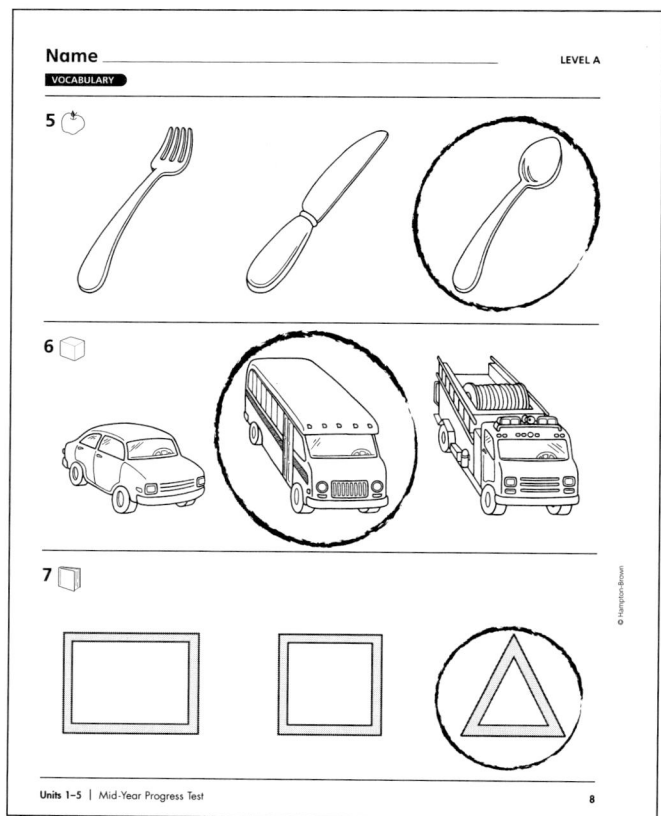

Answer Key • Mid-Year Progress Test

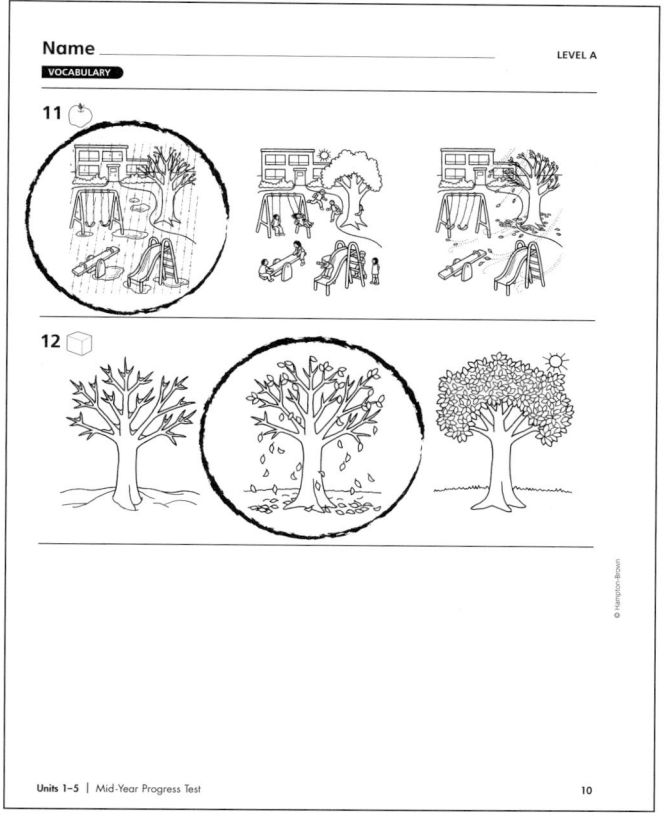

Answer Key • Mid-Year Progress Test

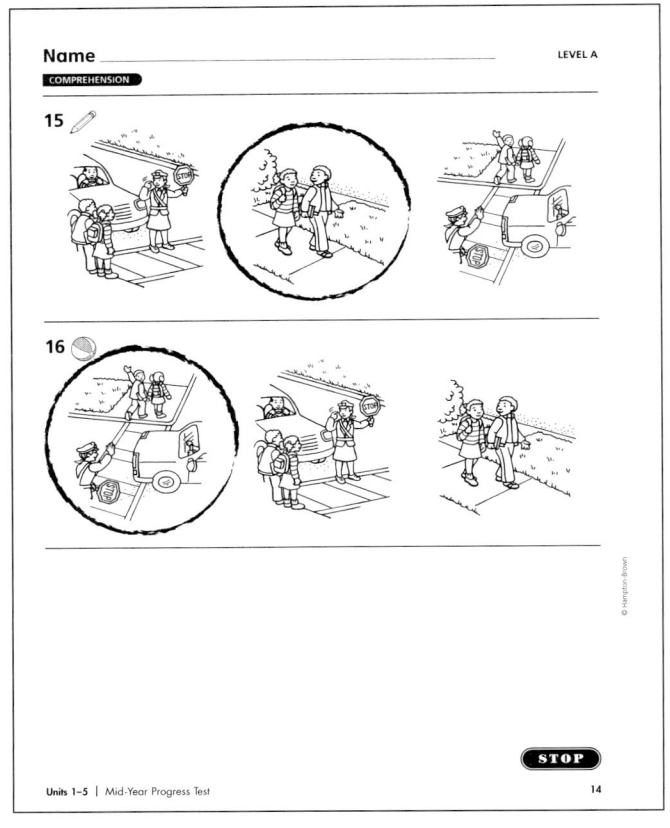

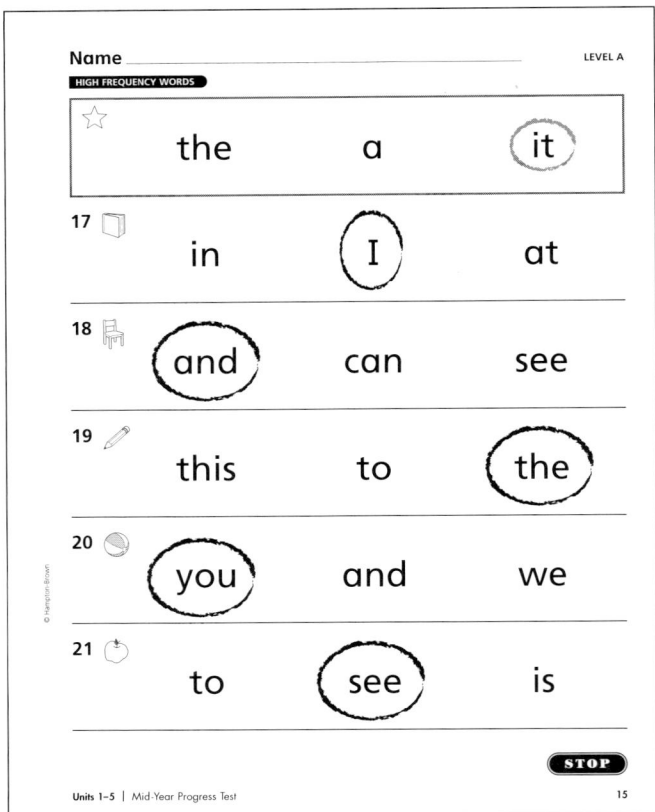

Units 1–5 | Answer Key

Units 6–10 • Directions for End-of-Year Progress Test

Administer the Progress Test in 2 or 3 sessions based on the attention span and level of your students—**Session 1:** Vocabulary; **Session 2:** Comprehension; **Session 3:** High Frequency Words. Administer the test on High Frequency Words only to advanced students who are learning to read in English.

Distribute pencils or crayons for circling answers. Draw a star on the board to help children locate the place to begin.

VOCABULARY

Distribute pages 23–27.

Sample
Put your finger on the star. Look at the pictures in the box. Find the crayon…crayon. *(Pause.) The first picture is the crayon. That's why there is a circle around the crayon.*

Items 1–12
Use the locator art to direct children from item to item. Repeat the directions using these prompts. Allow time for children to circle their answers.

1. *Find the* mouse…mouse.

Have children go to the next page.

2. *Find the* nest…nest.
3. *Find the girl pointing to her* ear…ear.
4. *Find the boy who is* sad…sad.

Have children go to the next page.

VOCABULARY continued

5. *Find the* horse…horse.
6. *Find the arrow in each picture. Which one points to the* lamb…lamb?
7. *Find the* apple…apple.

Have children go to the next page.

8. *Find the arrow in each picture. Which one points to the* flower…flower?
9. *Find the* dollar…dollar.
10. *Find the* sink…sink.

Have children go to the next page.

11. *Find the* house…house.
12. *Find the girl* waking up…waking up.

Units 6–10 • Directions for End-of-Year Progress Test

COMPREHENSION

Selection 1 and Items 13–14
Distribute page 28. Have children look at the page and follow along as you read the story. Direct children from picture to picture. Say: *Now listen to the story. The title is:*

Gloria's Salad Garden

Look at Picture 1. Look at the seeds.
Gloria plants the seeds.

Look at Picture 2. Look at the soil.
Gloria waters the soil.

Look at Picture 3. Look at the sprouts!
Gloria waters the sprouts.

Look at Picture 4. Gloria puts carrots, beans, peppers, and tomatoes in her salad.
Look at her eat!

Distribute page 29.

13. *Put your finger on the book. Look at the pictures. Listen to the question:* What does Gloria do first in the story? *Look at the pictures. Does she plant the seeds, eat a salad, or water the sprouts? Circle your answer.*

14. *Put your finger on the chair. Look at the pictures in the box. These are vegetables. Now look at the pictures under the box. Which one goes with the vegetables? Does the banana, potato, or pear go with the vegetables? Circle your answer.*

COMPREHENSION continued

Selection 2 and Items 15–16
Distribute page 30. Have children look at the page and follow along as you read the story. Direct children from picture to picture. Say: *Now listen to the story. The title is:*

A House for Pig

Look at Picture 1. Pig says to Cow, "I like your house. This is a big house."
"Moo," says Cow.

Look at Picture 2. Pig says to Cat, "I like your house. This is a big house."
"Meow," says Cat.

Look at Picture 3. Pig says to Puppy, "I like your house. This is a little house."
"Woof," says Puppy.

Look at Picture 4. Pig says to Hen, "I like your house. This is a little house."
"Cluck," says Hen.

Look at Picture 5. Pig says to Mama, "I like my house.
This is not a big house.
This is not a little house.
This is the place for me!"

Distribute page 31. Say:

15. *Put your finger on the pencil. Look at the pictures in the box. These are baby animals. Now look at the pictures under the box. Which one goes with the baby animals? Does the cow, the horse, or the puppy go with the baby animals? Circle your answer.*

16. *Put your finger on the ball. Look at the pictures. Two of the houses are little. One of the houses is big. Find the big house. Circle your answer.*

Units 6–10 • Directions for End-of-Year Progress Test

HIGH FREQUENCY WORDS

Distribute page 32. Say:

Sample
Put your finger on the star. Read the words. Find the word it. *Listen: I like* it. **(Pause.)** *The last word is* it. *That's why there is a circle around the word* it.

Items 17–21
Use the locator art to direct children from item to item. Repeat the directions using these words and context sentences. Allow time for children to circle their answers.

17. at…*I am* at *school.*
18. Where…*Where is my house?*
19. in…*I am* in *the kitchen.*
20. not…*This is* not *a pencil.*
21. Look…*Look at the butterfly.*

Units 6–10 | Directions

Student Profile • End-of-Year Progress Test

DIRECTIONS Record the child's name and test date. Use the **Answer Key** on pages 33–35 to score the child's test. Then, in the Student Profile, circle the item number of each correct answer and circle the plus or minus sign to indicate mastery. Calculate the subtest scores and then the total test score.

Student Name _____ Date _____

Subtest	Tested Skills	ITEM ANALYSIS		TEST SCORES
		Item Numbers	Mastery	No. Correct × Points = Score
VOCABULARY	Vocabulary from Units 6–10	1 2 3 4 5 6 7 8 9 10 11 12	10 out of 12 + −	_____ × 5 = ⬜/60
COMPREHENSION	Comprehension and Critical Thinking	13 14 15 16	3 out of 4 + −	_____ × 10 = ⬜/40
			TOTAL END-OF-YEAR PROGRESS TEST	⬜/100
FOR ADVANCED STUDENTS:				
LEARNING TO READ	High Frequency Words	17 18 19 20 21	4 out of 5 + −	

Units 6–10 | Student Profile   22

Name _____

LEVEL A

End-of-Year Progress Test

VOCABULARY

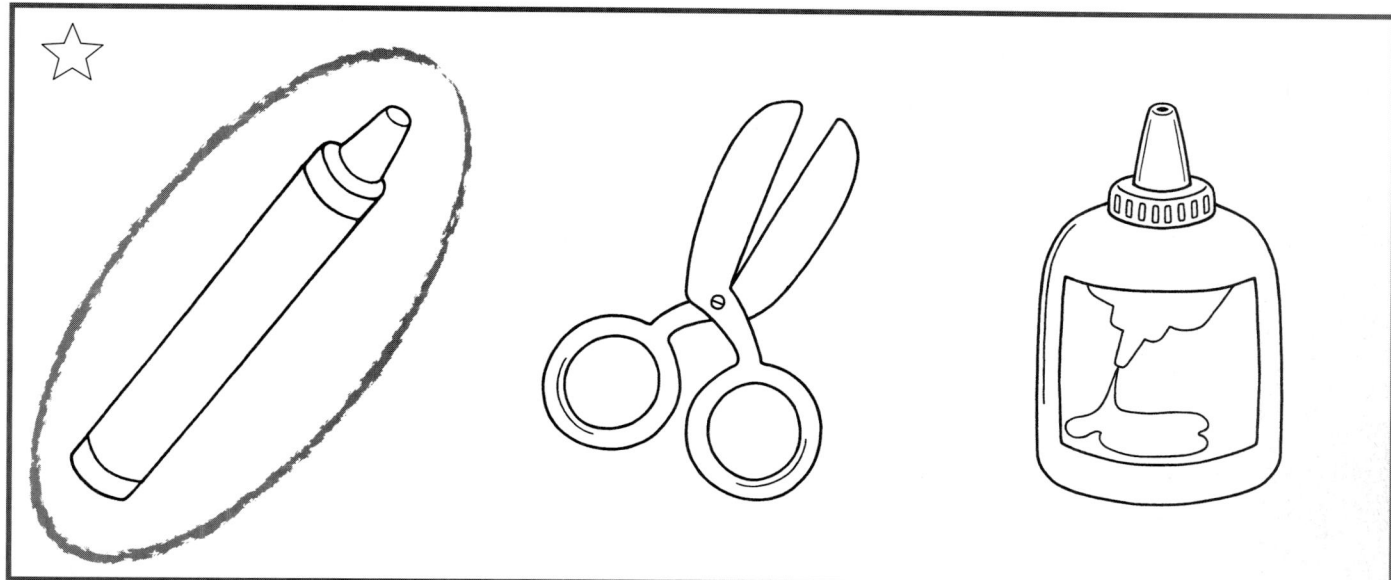

1 📖

Units 6–10 | End-of-Year Progress Test

Name

LEVEL A

VOCABULARY

2

3

4

Units 6–10 | End-of-Year Progress Test

Name

VOCABULARY

LEVEL A

5

6

7

  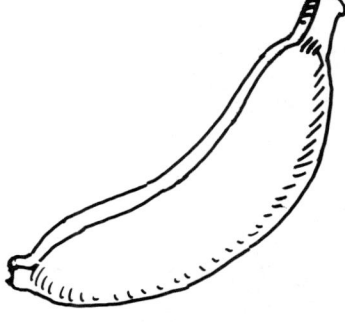

Units 6–10 | End-of-Year Progress Test

Name

LEVEL A

VOCABULARY

8

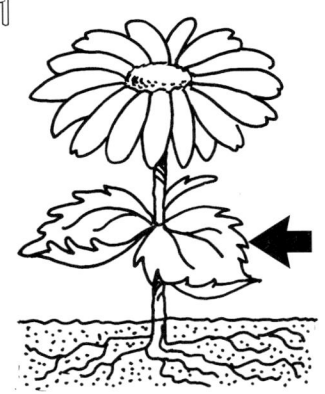 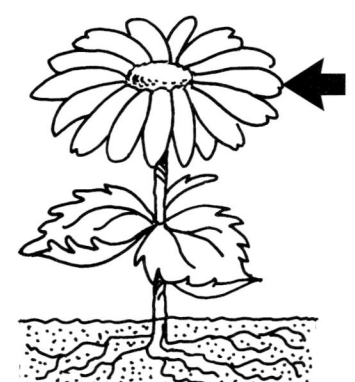 

9

10

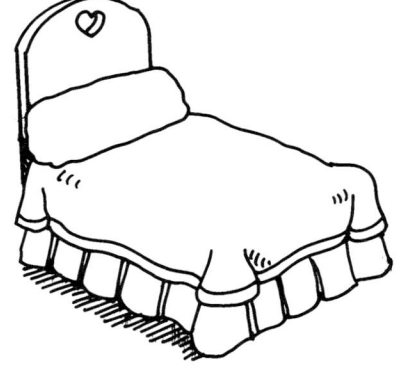  

Units 6–10 | End-of-Year Progress Test

Name

VOCABULARY

LEVEL A

11 🍎

12 ⬜

Units 6–10 | End-of-Year Progress Test

Name _____

LEVEL A

COMPREHENSION

Gloria's Salad Garden

Units 6–10 | End-of-Year Progress Test

Name

COMPREHENSION

LEVEL A

13 📖

14 🪑

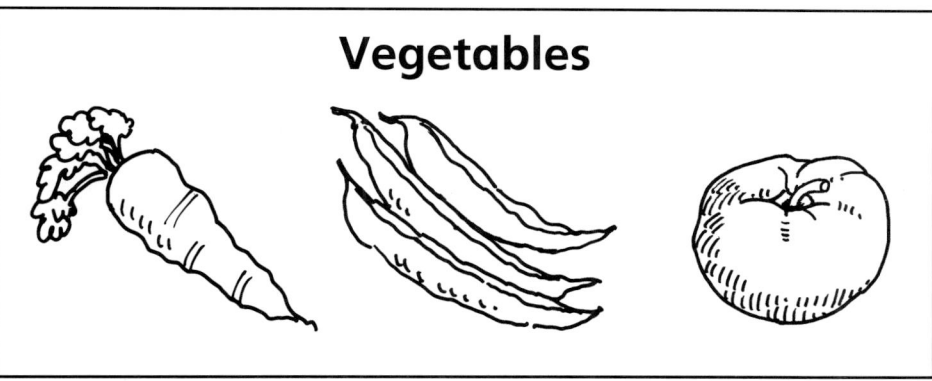

 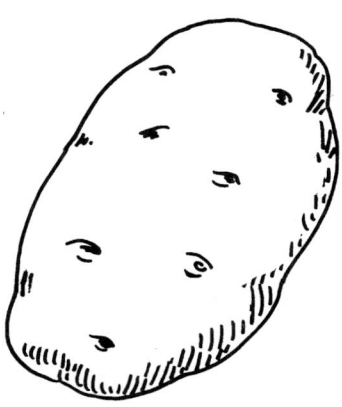 

A House for Pig

Name _____

LEVEL A

COMPREHENSION

15 ✏️

Baby Animals

16

STOP

Units 6–10 | End-of-Year Progress Test

Name _____ **LEVEL A**

HIGH FREQUENCY WORDS

| | the | a | (it) |

17   are   at   have

18   where   your   what

19   in   it   on

20   go   big   not

21   like   look   little

STOP

Units 6–10 | End-of-Year Progress Test 32

Answer Key • End-of-Year Progress Test

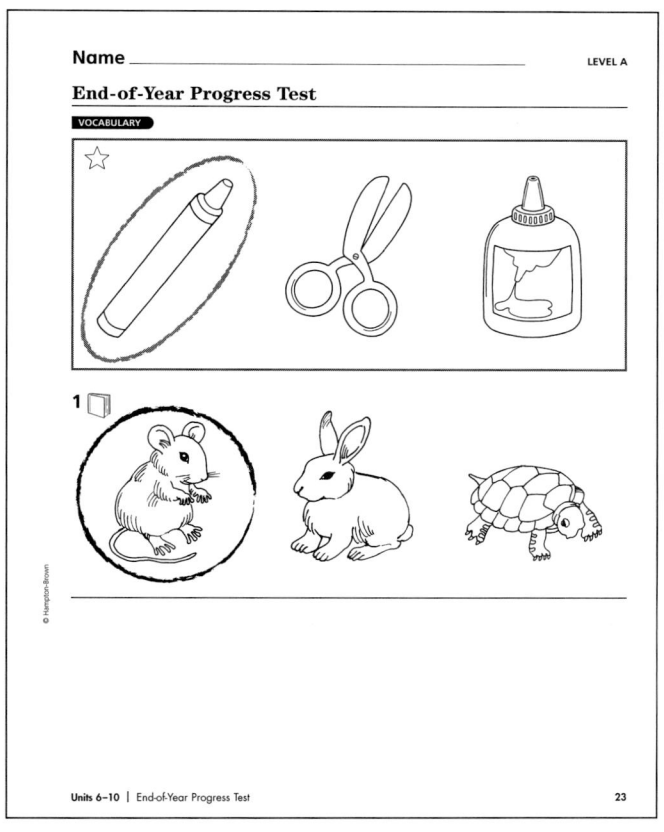

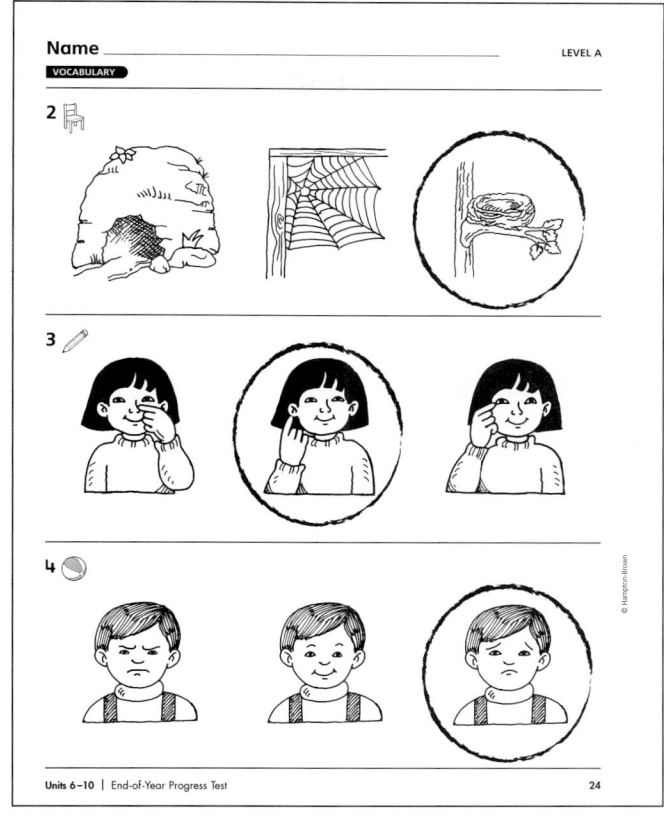

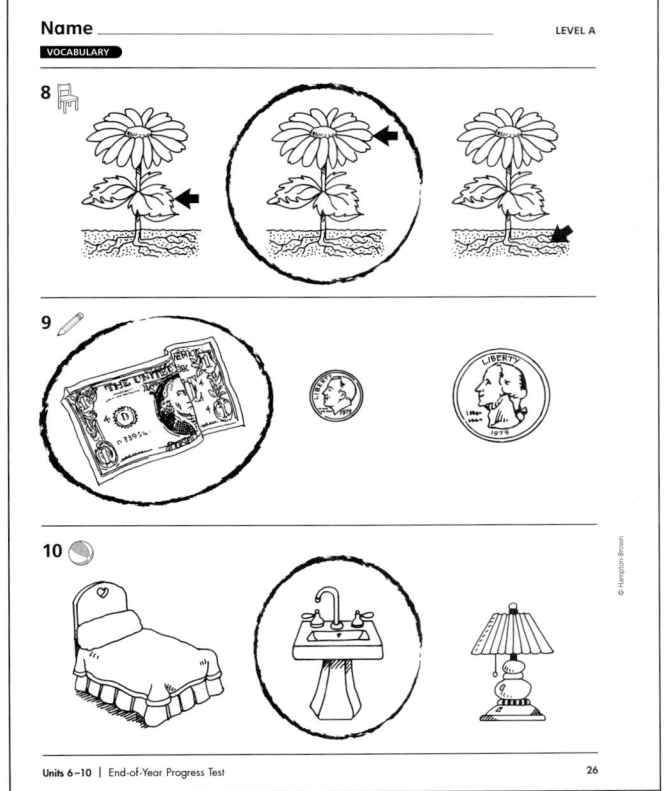

Units 6–10 | Answer Key

Answer Key • End-of-Year Progress Test

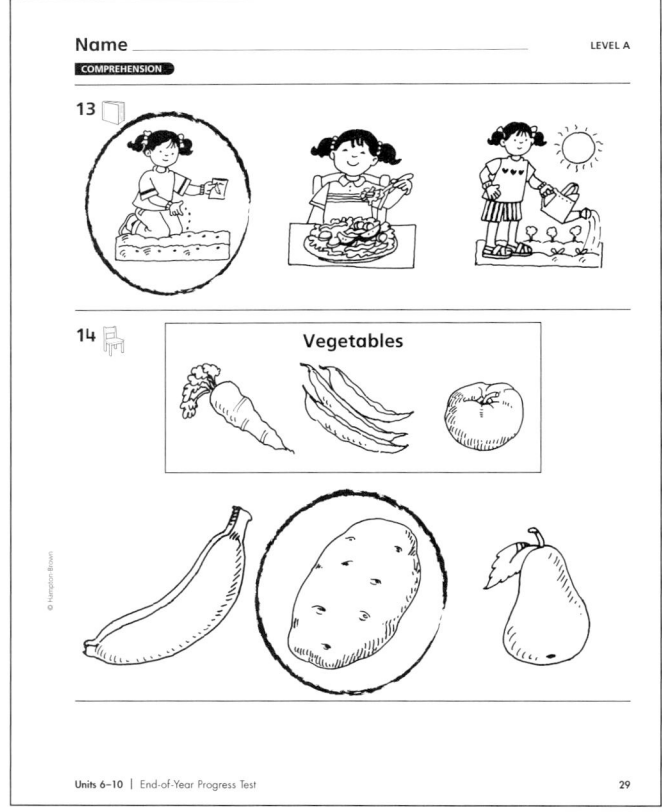

Answer Key • End-of-Year Progress Test

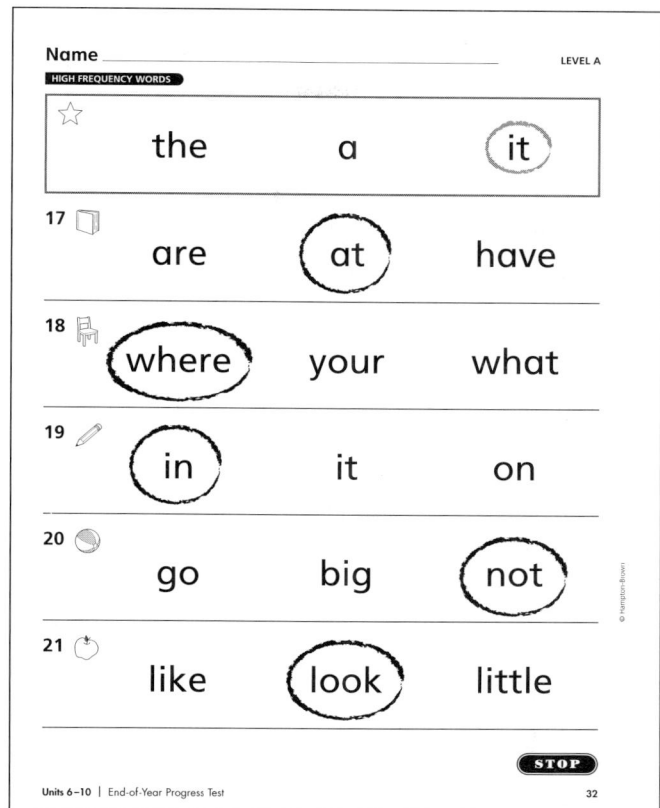

Performance Assessments

▶ **Vocabulary**

▶ **Language**

▶ **Concepts of Print**

Unit 1 • Vocabulary Assessment

DIRECTIONS Set up the activities described on Teacher's Edition page T44, at the end of Unit 1. Then form small groups. After you record each child's name, carry out the activity. Listen for children's use of the unit vocabulary and circle each word a child can point to or say in response to your prompts. Record additional comments.

Color Names — Date _____

Name	Vocabulary	Comments
	green blue yellow white red	
	green blue yellow white red	
	green blue yellow white red	
	green blue yellow white red	

School Tools — Date _____

Name	Vocabulary	Comments
	pencil book crayon glue scissors	
	pencil book crayon glue scissors	
	pencil book crayon glue scissors	
	pencil book crayon glue scissors	

Size Words — Date _____

Name	Vocabulary	Comments
	big small	
	big small	
	big small	
	big small	

School People — Date _____

Name	Vocabulary	Comments
	teacher librarian custodian bus driver crossing guard	
	teacher librarian custodian bus driver crossing guard	
	teacher librarian custodian bus driver crossing guard	
	teacher librarian custodian bus driver crossing guard	

© Hampton-Brown

Unit 2 • Vocabulary Assessment

DIRECTIONS Set up the activities described on Teacher's Edition page T88, at the end of Unit 2. Then form small groups. After you record each child's name, carry out the activity. Listen for children's use of the unit vocabulary and circle each word a child can point to or say in response to your prompts. Record additional comments.

Family Members Date _____

Name	Vocabulary	Comments
	mother father brother sister baby	
	mother father brother sister baby	
	mother father brother sister baby	
	mother father brother sister baby	

Food Names Date _____

Name	Vocabulary	Comments
	banana salad pizza chicken rice	
	banana salad pizza chicken rice	
	banana salad pizza chicken rice	
	banana salad pizza chicken rice	

Kitchen Objects Date _____

Name	Vocabulary	Comments
	plate fork knife spoon glass	
	plate fork knife spoon glass	
	plate fork knife spoon glass	
	plate fork knife spoon glass	

Number Words Date _____

Name	Vocabulary	Comments
	one two three four five	
	one two three four five	
	one two three four five	
	one two three four five	

Unit 3 • Vocabulary Assessment

DIRECTIONS Set up the activities described on Teacher's Edition page T132, at the end of Unit 3. Then form small groups. After you record each child's name, carry out the activity. Listen for children's use of the unit vocabulary and circle each word a child can point to or say in response to your prompts. Record additional comments.

Vehicle Names   Date _____

Name	Vocabulary	Comments
	bus train truck bike car	
	bus train truck bike car	
	bus train truck bike car	
	bus train truck bike car	

Vehicle Parts   Date _____

Name	Vocabulary	Comments
	seat window pedal wheel door	
	seat window pedal wheel door	
	seat window pedal wheel door	
	seat window pedal wheel door	

Shape Names   Date _____

Name	Vocabulary	Comments
	circle square triangle diamond	
	circle square triangle diamond	
	circle square triangle diamond	
	circle square triangle diamond	

Action Words   Date _____

Name	Vocabulary	Comments
	ride fly pull row drive	
	ride fly pull row drive	
	ride fly pull row drive	
	ride fly pull row drive	

© Hampton-Brown

Unit 4 • Vocabulary Assessment

DIRECTIONS Set up the activities described on Teacher's Edition page T176, at the end of Unit 4. Then form small groups. After you record each child's name, carry out the activity. Listen for children's use of the unit vocabulary and circle each word a child can point to or say in response to your prompts. Record additional comments.

Places Date _____

Name	Vocabulary	Comments
	post office restaurant fire station bakery grocery	
	post office restaurant fire station bakery grocery	
	post office restaurant fire station bakery grocery	
	post office restaurant fire station bakery grocery	

Workers Date _____

Name	Vocabulary	Comments
	doctor nurse letter carrier firefighter baker	
	doctor nurse letter carrier firefighter baker	
	doctor nurse letter carrier firefighter baker	
	doctor nurse letter carrier firefighter baker	

Opposites Date _____

Name	Vocabulary	Comments
	back/front full/empty open/closed over/under up/down	
	back/front full/empty open/closed over/under up/down	
	back/front full/empty open/closed over/under up/down	
	back/front full/empty open/closed over/under up/down	

Safety Words Date _____

Name	Vocabulary	Comments
	stop look listen crosswalk green light	
	stop look listen crosswalk green light	
	stop look listen crosswalk green light	
	stop look listen crosswalk green light	

© Hampton-Brown

Unit 5 • Vocabulary Assessment

DIRECTIONS Set up the activities described on Teacher's Edition page T220, at the end of Unit 5. Then form small groups. After you record each child's name, carry out the activity. Listen for children's use of the unit vocabulary and circle each word a child can point to or say in response to your prompts. Record additional comments.

Weather Words — Date _____

Name	Vocabulary	Comments
	sunny windy rainy snowy	
	sunny windy rainy snowy	
	sunny windy rainy snowy	
	sunny windy rainy snowy	

Action Words — Date _____

Name	Vocabulary	Comments
	ride hide swim dig rake	
	ride hide swim dig rake	
	ride hide swim dig rake	
	ride hide swim dig rake	

Seasons — Date _____

Name	Vocabulary	Comments
	spring summer fall winter	
	spring summer fall winter	
	spring summer fall winter	
	spring summer fall winter	

Clothing Names — Date _____

Name	Vocabulary	Comments
	raincoat sweater boots jacket sandals	
	raincoat sweater boots jacket sandals	
	raincoat sweater boots jacket sandals	
	raincoat sweater boots jacket sandals	

© Hampton-Brown

Unit 6 • Vocabulary Assessment

DIRECTIONS Set up the activities described on Teacher's Edition page T44, at the end of Unit 6. Then form small groups. After you record each child's name, carry out the activity. Listen for children's use of the unit vocabulary and circle each word a child can point to or say in response to your prompts. Record additional comments.

Wild Animals   Date _____

Name	Vocabulary	Comments
	whale elephant lion owl snake	
	whale elephant lion owl snake	
	whale elephant lion owl snake	
	whale elephant lion owl snake	

Pets   Date _____

Name	Vocabulary	Comments
	dog frog cat fish bird	
	dog frog cat fish bird	
	dog frog cat fish bird	
	dog frog cat fish bird	

Animal Body Parts   Date _____

Name	Vocabulary	Comments
	tail wing feathers fur scales	
	tail wing feathers fur scales	
	tail wing feathers fur scales	
	tail wing feathers fur scales	

Animal Homes   Date _____

Name	Vocabulary	Comments
	nest web den cave	
	nest web den cave	
	nest web den cave	
	nest web den cave	

© Hampton-Brown

Unit 7 • Vocabulary Assessment

DIRECTIONS Set up the activities described on Teacher's Edition page T88, at the end of Unit 7. Then form small groups. After you record each child's name, carry out the activity. Listen for children's use of the unit vocabulary and circle each word a child can point to or say in response to your prompts. Record additional comments.

Actions Date _____

Name	Vocabulary	Comments
	hop / slide / climb / dig / jump	
	hop / slide / climb / dig / jump	
	hop / slide / climb / dig / jump	
	hop / slide / climb / dig / jump	

Parts of the Body Date _____

Name	Vocabulary	Comments
	hand / foot / eye / ear / nose	
	hand / foot / eye / ear / nose	
	hand / foot / eye / ear / nose	
	hand / foot / eye / ear / nose	

Words for Senses Date _____

Name	Vocabulary	Comments
	hear / see / smell / taste / touch	
	hear / see / smell / taste / touch	
	hear / see / smell / taste / touch	
	hear / see / smell / taste / touch	

Words for Feelings Date _____

Name	Vocabulary	Comments
	angry / happy / surprised / sad	
	angry / happy / surprised / sad	
	angry / happy / surprised / sad	
	angry / happy / surprised / sad	

© Hampton-Brown

Unit 8 • Vocabulary Assessment

DIRECTIONS Set up the activities described on Teacher's Edition page T132, at the end of Unit 8. Then form small groups. After you record each child's name, carry out the activity. Listen for children's use of the unit vocabulary and circle each word a child can point to or say in response to your prompts. Record additional comments.

Farm Animals		Date _____	Baby Animals		Date _____
Name	**Vocabulary**	**Comments**	**Name**	**Vocabulary**	**Comments**
	chicken pig goose cow horse			kitten puppy piglet chick calf	
	chicken pig goose cow horse			kitten puppy piglet chick calf	
	chicken pig goose cow horse			kitten puppy piglet chick calf	
	chicken pig goose cow horse			kitten puppy piglet chick calf	

Words for Where		Date _____	Animal Life Cycles		Date _____
Name	**Vocabulary**	**Comments**	**Name**	**Vocabulary**	**Comments**
	in on over under			egg hatch caterpillar butterfly	
	in on over under			egg hatch caterpillar butterfly	
	in on over under			egg hatch caterpillar butterfly	
	in on over under			egg hatch caterpillar butterfly	

Unit 9 • Vocabulary Assessment

DIRECTIONS Set up the activities described on Teacher's Edition page T176, at the end of Unit 9. Then form small groups. After you record each child's name, carry out the activity. Listen for children's use of the unit vocabulary and circle each word a child can point to or say in response to your prompts. Record additional comments.

Fruits / Vegetables   Date _____

Name	Vocabulary	Comments
	carrot potato apple orange tomato	
	carrot potato apple orange tomato	
	carrot potato apple orange tomato	
	carrot potato apple orange tomato	

Plant Life Cycles   Date _____

Name	Vocabulary	Comments
	seed leaf stem root flower	
	seed leaf stem root flower	
	seed leaf stem root flower	
	seed leaf stem root flower	

Farm to Table   Date _____

Name	Vocabulary	Comments
	orange tree orange juice wheat field bread	
	orange tree orange juice wheat field bread	
	orange tree orange juice wheat field bread	
	orange tree orange juice wheat field bread	

Buying and Selling   Date _____

Name	Vocabulary	Comments
	penny nickel dime dollar	
	penny nickel dime dollar	
	penny nickel dime dollar	
	penny nickel dime dollar	

Unit 10 • Vocabulary Assessment

DIRECTIONS Set up the activities described on Teacher's Edition page T220, at the end of Unit 10. Then form small groups. After you record each child's name, carry out the activity. Listen for children's use of the unit vocabulary and circle each word a child can point to or say in response to your prompts. Record additional comments.

Rooms in a Home — Date _____

Name	Vocabulary	Comments
	living room bathroom bedroom kitchen	
	living room bathroom bedroom kitchen	
	living room bathroom bedroom kitchen	
	living room bathroom bedroom kitchen	

Household Objects — Date _____

Name	Vocabulary	Comments
	couch bed sink chair lamp	
	couch bed sink chair lamp	
	couch bed sink chair lamp	
	couch bed sink chair lamp	

Kinds of Homes — Date _____

Name	Vocabulary	Comments
	apartment house log cabin mobile home tent	
	apartment house log cabin mobile home tent	
	apartment house log cabin mobile home tent	
	apartment house log cabin mobile home tent	

Daily Routines — Date _____

Name	Vocabulary	Comments
	sleep brush teeth breakfast lunch dinner	
	sleep brush teeth breakfast lunch dinner	
	sleep brush teeth breakfast lunch dinner	
	sleep brush teeth breakfast lunch dinner	

Name _____

Language Assessments

SHOW ME SCHOOL TOOLS

Date _____

USE AFTER UNIT 1

- Language Function:
  Give and Carry Out Commands
- **ACTIVITY:** Display a crayon, a book, a pair of scissors, and some paper. Have children follow your commands. Say: *Please give me the crayon. Cut the paper with the scissors. Point to the book.* Then have each child give you commands. Check the box in the Rubric that most closely matches your observation.

Rubric

- ☐ **BEGINNING** Responds and gives commands nonverbally using gestures and pointing.
- ☐ **INTERMEDIATE** Follows commands accurately and uses fragments or simple sentences to give commands (*give crayon, cut paper, point book*).
- ☐ **ADVANCED** Follows commands accurately. Begins each command with a verb. Uses appropriate intonation to give commands.

WHAT DO YOU LIKE?

Date _____

USE AFTER UNIT 2

- Language Function:
  Express Likes and Dislikes
- **ACTIVITY:** Display four **Food Manipulatives** from Unit 2. Name each food; then sort them as you verbalize: *I like pizza. I do not like green beans.* Hold up each card in turn and say: *Tell me how you feel about (pizza).* Check the box in the Rubric that most closely matches your observation.

Rubric

- ☐ **BEGINNING** Uses facial expressions and/or nods "yes" or "no" to show likes and dislikes.
- ☐ **INTERMEDIATE** Uses fragments or simple sentences with errors (*Yes, pizza. I no like green beans.*).
- ☐ **ADVANCED** Uses complete sentences (*I like _____; I do not like _____.*).

Name _____

Language Assessments

LOOK AT THE CAR GO!

Date _____

USE AFTER UNIT 3

Rubric

- **Language Function:**
  Give and Follow Directions
- **ACTIVITY:** Display a toy car and truck or the **Vehicle Manipulatives** from Unit 3 on a table or desk. Say: *Hold up the car. Put the car on the desk. Push the car across the desk.* Then have each child give you directions. Check the box in the Rubric that most closely matches your observation.

- ☐ **BEGINNING** Moves the car appropriately to show understanding of the directions. Uses gestures or pantomimes to give directions.
- ☐ **INTERMEDIATE** Successfully follows the directions and uses simple sentences with a few errors to give directions *(Hold up car. Put on desk. Push.)*.
- ☐ **ADVANCED** Accurately follows the directions and repeats them or gives new directions with few or no errors.

ARE THEY ALIKE OR DIFFERENT?

Date _____

USE AFTER UNIT 4 OR 5

Rubric

- **Language Function:**
  Make Comparisons
- **ACTIVITY:** Display two red crayons, one shorter than the other. Ask children: *How are these the same?* (Both are red. Both are crayons.) *How are the crayons different?* (This/That one is shorter/longer.) Check the box in the Rubric that most closely matches your observation.

- ☐ **BEGINNING** Uses gestures or single words to identify points of comparison *(red, crayons; short, long)*.
- ☐ **INTERMEDIATE** Uses simple phrases with comparative words and few errors *(Both red; red crayons; is shorter)*.
- ☐ **ADVANCED** Uses complete sentences and comparative words *(Both crayons are red. This crayon is shorter than that crayon.)*.

TELL ABOUT THE ANIMALS

Date _____

USE AFTER UNIT 6

Rubric

- **Language Function:**
  Give Information
- **ACTIVITY:** Display the **Animal Manipulatives** from Unit 6. Have each child choose an animal. Then say: *Tell me the name of your animal.* (Pause.) *Tell me one thing it has. Tell me what it is like.* Check the box in the Rubric that most closely matches your observation.

- ☐ **BEGINNING** Points to and names the animal. Points to one feature (ears, tail, etc.) and acts out what the animal is like.
- ☐ **INTERMEDIATE** Uses short phrases and simple sentences with a few errors to name the animal and give information about it *(Fish. Has fins. Little.)*.
- ☐ **ADVANCED** Uses complete sentences with details to give information about the animal *(This is a giraffe. It has a long neck. It is tall.)*.

Language Assessments

Name _____

Language Assessments

ASK ME, TELL ME

Date _____

USE AFTER UNIT 7

Rubric

- **Language Function:**
  Ask for and Give Information
- **ACTIVITY:** Sketch a picture. Ask: *What is it?* After children guess, model, *Yes, it is a _____.* Have partners take turns drawing and talking about their pictures. Listen as children ask about and tell about the pictures. Check the box in the Rubric that most closely matches your observation.

- ☐ **BEGINNING** Uses gestures and words to ask and tell about a picture *(What? flower).*
- ☐ **INTERMEDIATE** Asks a question and uses complete sentences with errors to name or give a detail about a picture *(What is it? Is flower.).*
- ☐ **ADVANCED** Asks a question and uses complete sentences to name the picture and add one or more details *(What is it? It is a yellow flower.).*

HOW DO YOU FEEL?

Date _____

USE AFTER UNIT 7

Rubric

- **Language Function:**
  Express Feelings
- **ACTIVITY:** Display the **Language Songs Big Book** page 7B. Point to each photo in turn as you say: *Look at the boy (girl). Pretend you are the boy (girl). How do you feel? How are you? Why?* Listen for feeling words as the child responds. Check the box in the Rubric that most closely matches your observation.

- ☐ **BEGINNING** Responds nonverbally, using facial expressions and body language, or uses single feeling words (happy, angry, surprised, sad).
- ☐ **INTERMEDIATE** Uses simple sentences with errors *(I happy.).*
- ☐ **ADVANCED** Uses complete sentences *(I feel/am happy today.).*

Name _____

Language Assessments

I LIKE IT!

Date _____

USE AFTER UNIT 8

- **Language Function:**
  Express Likes and Dislikes
- **ACTIVITY:** Draw a picture of something you like and a picture of something you don't like. (You can also use the **Picture Cards** or the **Manipulatives**.) Display each picture as you verbalize: *I like* _____. *I do not like* _____. Then have each child draw or select pictures to express likes and dislikes. Check the box in the Rubric that most closely matches your observation.

Rubric

- ☐ **BEGINNING** Uses facial expressions or gestures and says "yes" (for *like*) or "no" (for *do not like*) as she or he displays each picture.
- ☐ **INTERMEDIATE** Uses complete sentences with a few errors to express likes and dislikes *(I like pizza. I no like salad.)*.
- ☐ **ADVANCED** Uses complete sentences to express likes and dislikes *(I like corn. I do not/don't like green beans.)*.

GIVE A HOME TOUR

Date _____

USE AFTER UNIT 10

- **Language Function:**
  Give Information
- **ACTIVITY:** Display the **Vocabulary Builder 10** and the **Furniture Manipulatives**. Then say: *Tell me what this is.* (Pause.) *Tell me where it goes in a home. Tell me what you do with it.* Check the box in the Rubric that most closely matches your observation.

Rubric

- ☐ **BEGINNING** Names the item. Shows or points to the furniture's location in a house. Demonstrates its functions with gestures.
- ☐ **INTERMEDIATE** Uses short phrases and simple sentences with a few errors to name the item and give information about it *(Sofa. In living room. Sit.)*.
- ☐ **ADVANCED** Uses complete sentences with details to give information about the item *(This is a sofa. It goes in the living room. We sit on it.)*.

Concepts-of-Print Assessment

Test and Student Profile

DIRECTIONS Select a short book from the classroom library. Use the Scripted Instructions in the middle column to administer each test item. Circle the score for each correct response; mark the score with an X for each incorrect response. Record the total score in the Student Profile chart.

Student Profile		
Test Date	Score /15	Percent %
Test Date	Score /15	Percent %
Test Date	Score /15	Percent %

Student Name _____

Objectives	Scripted Instructions	Score	
1. The student identifies the front and back covers of a book.	Holding the book vertically, spine outward, pass the book to the child. Say: *Show me the front of the book. Show me the back.*	Student points to the front and back covers.	1
2. The student identifies the title of a book.	Say: *Where is the title of the book? Show it to me.*	Student points to the title.	1
3. The student finds the title and author on the title page.	Say: *Look at the first page. Show me the title of the book. Show me the name of the person who wrote the book.*	Student points to: title author	1 1
4. The student recognizes that print provides information.	Say: *Look at these pages. Show me where the story starts.*	Student points to first word in text (not illustration).	1
5. The student tracks print from left to right and top to bottom on a page.	Say: *Now I'm going to read the book. Which way do I go as I read?* Read to the end of a line on a page with multiple lines. Then say: *Where do I go from here?*	Student indicates left-to-right tracking. Student indicates diagonal left return sweep.	1 1
6. The student matches oral and printed words.	Continue reading. Pause before reading a page. Say: *On this page, point to each word as I say it.*	Student points to each word you read.	1
7. The student identifies sentences.	Pause after reading a declarative sentence. Point to the period and say: *What is this for?* Continue reading and pause after a question. Point to the question mark and say: *What is this for?*	Student notes that a period ends a sentence. Student notes that a question mark comes at the end of a sentence that asks a question.	1 1
8. The student recognizes that sentences are composed of separate words. (Word Boundaries)	Read to the end of the book. On the last page, frame a sentence and say: *Use your finger to point to each word in this sentence. Count the words.*	Student points to each word in the sentence and counts the words.	1
9. The student recognizes the difference between letters and words.	Say: *Point to the first letter in this word. Point to the last letter.*	Student points to: first letter in the word last letter in the word	1 1
10. The student recognizes capital and lowercase letters.	Point out a capital letter and say: *This is a capital letter* [T]. *Find a small letter* [t]. Repeat for one additional letter.	Student finds a lowercase letter that matches the capital. Student makes another match.	1 1
			/15

© Hampton-Brown

Concepts-of-Print Assessment & Student Profile